Morning Dives

Volume 1

Morning Dives Vol. 1 Artistic Team
D.C. Kinder: Coordinator
Syed Saboorali
Formatting and editing
Nurul Huda:
Cover and background artist
D.C. Kinder:
Image design editing

Table Of Contents

Introduction 1

God's Unconditional Love, With Conditions 2

Jesus, the Master Swordsman vs Satan, the Master Deceiver 4

God will Come through for You in Time of Need 9

Flickers of Fire in a Flood of Forgetfulness 12

"Heart Shields Up,Captain" 14

Wisdom vs Folly 16

No Secrets Allowed 18

Really 20

Deep Waters 21

Woe is Me, So is Me 23

Who's Our Landlord? 25

Chosen, But You Must Choose 27

Come On. 29

The Great Custody Battle Pt 1 31

The Great Custody Battle 33

Comfort is More than Food 36

Written On My Heart 38

Someone Turn the Light On! 41

"Battle Stations" 44

The Way of Suffering, the Path of Glory 46
For me to live is What? 48
Steady as She Goes 50
The Path to Leadership 52
Death Destroyed 54
Missing in Action 56
Out of Nowhere, Kindness Appeared 58
"Hello, who's this?" 60
The Cure for Death 62
The Taste of Death 64
Tug of War 66
Get At Peace With God Now, or There will be No Resting in Peace Later 68
Christ, Our Designated Hitter 70
End of Morning Dives 72
Conclusion 72
Author Bio 74

Introduction

Tired of showing up at church and just being religious, watching friends fall asleep out of boredom without paying much attention. Maybe, it's time for a morning workout. You can take a refreshing morning dive into the Bible. Afterward, you'll be refreshed and ready to start your day off with real power, ready to face whatever comes your way, and ready to make whatever changes you need to make. You can put God's word into action like never before.

So, climb out of bed, and dive headfirst into God's powerful word. Even if you've never cracked a Bible before, you can come away with some awesome lessons to start your day. So grab up this book, and let it set you on the right path, one day at a time, one dive at a time, or maybe two dives, if you can't get enough.

"Your word is a lamp for my feet, a light on my path."

Psalms 119:105 NIV

So, turn the light on every morning, and let God's word light up your life, as you dive in. Enjoy your day.

God's Unconditional Love, With Conditions

Matthew 7:13, 14

Most people know that God's love is unconditional. It extends to all mankind no matter where they live or what they do. He gives them rain and blessings.

Most people forget that his favor, his peace, his forgiveness, his partnership, his salvation, his promise of eternal life with his presence are not unconditional.

Although God's unconditional love covers everyone, Jesus said that only a few will find their way to eternal life.

13 "Enter through the narrow gate. For wide is the gate and broad is the road that leads to destruction, and many enter through it. **14** But small is the gate and narrow the road that leads to life, and only a few find it. Matt 7:13, 14

We still have the freedom to chose our path. We are all free to hear the message. We are free to respond to it, or not.

While many people pour out their wants to God, few actually ask the question that the demon possessed man did in Matthew 8.

"When he saw Jesus, he cried out and fell at his feet, shouting at the top of his voice, "What do you want with me, Jesus, Son of the Most High God? I beg you, don't torture me!""

Luke 8:28 NIV

If we think that Jesus is out to burden and torture us, there's a good chance that this same demon is at work on our hearts. In truth, Jesus has come to set us free. That's what happened to this poor man. Jesus drove out the demon, and the man got back his right mind, the mind that loves God and wants to be close to him.

"and the people went out to see what had happened. When they came to Jesus, they found the man from whom the demons had gone out, sitting at Jesus' feet, dressed and in his right mind; and they were afraid."

Luke 8:35 NIV

Any other mind is not the right mind. If we don't desire with all of our hearts to be with Jesus and other disciples, we are not in our right minds. We are attracted to the other things of the world, temporary pleasures that feel great, but only for a short time.

Charge

Let's go out today remembering that we need to respond to God's wide open hands. Let us come to him with our wide open hearts, and he will gladly give us his heart, as well. We should never take him for granted.

Response Notes

Jesus, the Master Swordsman vs Satan, the Master Deceiver

Matthew 4 and Luke 4:1-13

These chapters bring us ringside to a Championship Match like no other. In this corner, we have Satan, the Father of lies, the Master of Disasters who took out 24,000 Israelites in one day. Numbers 25. In the other corner, we have the young faithful man/God named Jesus armed with his simple faith in God, and his dependance on him for all things even after a 40 day fast.

Will this young man stand up to the challenge, or will he go down in the first round against his cunning opponent? Satan has been known to bend and even break the rules whenever he can get away with it.

The bell rings as Jesus is led by the Spirit into the desert wilderness. Matt 4:1, Luke 4:1

Round 1

Hit'em Where It Hurts

After fasting forty days and forty nights, he was hungry. The tempter came to him and said, "If you are the Son of God, tell these stones to become bread."

Matthew 4:2-3 NIV

Satan comes out of his corner in a rage and immediately goes for a sucker punch hitting him where it hurts. Seeing that Jesus has been fasting for some time, he sees an opening to pull out one of his oldest tricks. Go for the worldly appetites. It worked so well in the wilderness against the Israelites that they were ready to stone Moses over a little food and drink. Later, he got them again with those delectable Moabite women who they couldn't resist. "Instant gratification would surely bring this would be Son of God down to his knees," Satan thought. "It worked so well with Adam and Eve, and countless hungry souls after that."

Back to the match, the crowd watches in shock as Jesus is hit hard by this temptation and falls against the ropes. Everyone gasps, wondering if he is gonna fall after such a powerful calculated assault.

"Jesus answered, "It is written: 'Man shall not live on bread alone, but on every word that comes from the mouth of God.' ""

Matthew 4:4 NIV

Jesus comes back with a hard right to the face. He could have given in so easily and made bread outta some stones wasting his power to prove his identity. Jesus already knew he was the Son of God. He was not going to break his fast until he was ready to. He was not fooled by the tempter's offer for a quick taste of fast food. Jesus reserved his strength to feed five thousand hungry souls rather than indulge himself on Satan's junk food.

"Boom," Satan is knocked clean across the ring, stunned by Jesus' knowledge of God's word and the speed of his quick reply. Satan was going to have to come up with a new strategy in round 2, if he was going to win this fight.

Round 2

It's Show-time!

Satan comes growling out of his corner and slams Jesus with an upper cut knocking him to the top of the temple. From there, he could see the courtyard where he would spend hours confronting the Jewish people trying to open their eyes to the fact that he was the Son of God. It was there that they would even threaten to stone him.

Satan continued to pound Jesus with powerful combinations if punches challenging Jesus' very identity.

"Then the devil took him to the holy city and had him stand on the highest point of the temple. "If you are the Son of God," he said, "throw yourself down. For it is written: " 'He will command his angels concerning you, and they will lift you up in their hands, so that you will not strike your foot against a stone.' "

Matthew 4:5-6 NIV

Jesus looked over the people on the ground in the temple and contemplated what they would think as they would see the angels catch him to stop his fall. They would all have to believe, and most importantly their path to faith would to instant, without him having to go to the cross. Stunned by Satan's relentless attack, Jesus quickly came back with a counterpunch.

"Jesus answered him, "It is also written: 'Do not put the Lord your God to the test.' "

Matthew 4:7 NIV

Jesus realized that this was just another one of Satan's dangerous short cut scam offers. Jesus knew that God's path of life is never the same as the wide easy road. He would not put on a show for anyone that did not involve the cross, and he would certainly not put God to the test by placing demands on God instead of humble prayers. How often we lose faith because we demand God act on our schedule instead of his. How we think things should turn out and how God wants things to go down are often not even close.

Satan was again knocked across the ring, and this time knocked off his feet. Quickly, he got up and pulled something out of his sleeve. He was ready for round three.

Round 3

Is That Your Final Answer?

Once again, Satan comes out, this time dancing across the ring, circling Jesus with his fancy footwork. "Boom he lands another uppercut just when Jesus turned his other cheek. This time Satan knocked him clean to the highest mountain in the region with a view that was something to behold.

"Again, the devil took him to a very high mountain and showed him all the kingdoms of the world and their splendor. "All this I will give you," he said, "if you will bow down and worship me.""

Matthew 4:8-9 NIV

Satan had hit hard with his, "you can have it all," sales pitch. We know it as the "you don't have to, take it easy" approach to life. Jesus knew that he was to be the King of the Jews, and eventually, the King of all nations with all authority given to him, but that would be on the other side of the cross. Satan was offering another easy less painful way to Kingship. Still it was stunning seeing all the splendor of the Kingdoms of the world laid out in front of him. It could all be his, if he would just bow down. There was not even a down payment or easy payment plan. Quickly, Jesus saw through the duplicity of this phony offer because he knew that his Father was the true ruler of this world. Jesus got back up and with one final blow he ended this Match with a resounding victory.

"Jesus said to him, "Away from me, Satan! For it is written: 'Worship the Lord your God, and serve him only.' " Then the devil left him, and angels came and attended him."

Matthew 4:10-11 NIV

The Winner of this match was Jesus winning all 3 rounds. Jesus even told the Devil to get lost after clearly trouncing him. But he would come back every chance he got. Luke 4:13

We must always keep in mind that Satan, even now, wants to take us out when he tempts us with sin.

Challenge

Let's go out today, remembering that we too can have victory over sin and evil because we too can have the mind of Christ to overcome.

1 Corinthians 2:16

Today, let's knock sin and Satan out of the park.

Notes

God will Come through for You in Time of Need.

He is Able to Deliver (Joshua)

We loves those movies where the hero, or the Calvary arrive just in time to rescue the hostages, or the wagon train, or the person tied to a bomb.

The question remains, who is going to deliver us?

Here are some encouraging verses found in the book of Joshua. They are matched up to similar verses in the New Testament. God always looks after his people.

God's people share with those in need.

"The inheritance of the Simeonites was taken from the share of Judah, because Judah's portion was more than they needed. So the Simeonites received their inheritance within the territory of Judah."

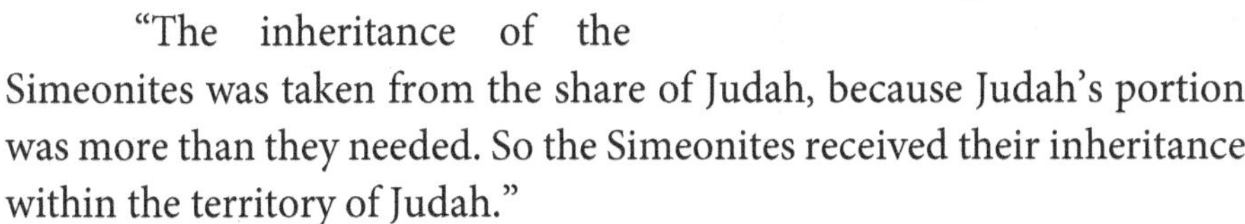

Joshua 19:9 NIV

"They sold property and possessions to give to anyone who had need."

Acts 2:45 NIV

God's people trust in his promises.

"Not one of all the Lord's good promises to Israel failed; every one was fulfilled."

Joshua 21:45

"Through these he has given us his very great and precious promises, so that through them you may participate in the divine nature, having escaped the corruption in the world caused by evil desires."

2 Peter 1:4 NIV

God always delivers those who are his.

Joshua 21:45 NIV

"One of you routs a thousand, because the Lord your God fights for you, just as he promised. So be very careful to love the Lord your God."

Joshua 23:10-11 NIV

"No temptation has overtaken you except what is common to mankind. And God is faithful; he will not let you be tempted beyond what you can bear. But when you are tempted, he will also provide a way out so that you can endure it."

1 Corinthians 10:13 NIV

"Indeed, we felt we had received the sentence of death. But this happened that we might not rely on ourselves but on God, who raises the dead. He has delivered us from such a deadly peril, and he will deliver us again. On him we have set our hope that he will continue to deliver us,"

2 Corinthians 1:9-10

“Who shall separate us from the love of Christ? Shall trouble or hardship or persecution or famine or nakedness or danger or sword? No, in all these things we are more than conquerors through him who loved us. For I am convinced that neither death nor life, neither angels nor demons, neither the present nor the future, nor any powers, neither height nor depth, nor anything else in all creation, will be able to separate us from the love of God that is in Christ Jesus our Lord.”

Romans 8:35, 37-39

Challenge

As we go out today, let’s reflect on who are we relying on to deliver us. Do we really believe that we can get it together on our own power? We can’t even control what happens tomorrow. If we are lucky, we will make it home from work today.

Flickers of Fire in a Flood of Forgetfulness

Judges to the Rescue, 3-6

We recall that soon after the death of Joshua and his team of leaders, the people of God start to join up with the remaining peoples and forget their amazing God who brought them out of slavery. They would prefer to just blend in with the nations rather than stand up and stand out with their God.

"They were left to test the Israelites to see whether they would obey the Lord's commands, which he had given their ancestors through Moses. The Israelites lived among the Canaanites, Hittites, Amorites, Perizzites, Hivites and Jebusites. They took their daughters in marriage and gave their own daughters to their sons, and served their gods."

Judges 3:4-6 NIV

The first Judge was Othniel, Caleb's nephew. He, like his Uncle, carried the torch of faith for 40 years and brought peace to the land. "So the land had peace for forty years, until Othniel son of Kenaz died."

Judges 3:11 NIV

"Again the Israelites did evil in the eyes of the Lord, and because they did this evil the Lord gave Eglon king of Moab power over Israel."

Judges 3:12 NIV

Here we go again. The fog of forgetfulness prevails and once again, people set their hearts on evil. Until Ehud comes along and begins a faithful battle that sets the people free once more.

"That day Moab was made subject to Israel, and the land had peace for eighty years."

Judges 3:30

After him, came Shamgar, who defeated the Philistines. Then Deborah arose to free her people from the oppression of King Jabin and the Canaanites. She and her co-leader Barak marched off to battle a powerful army of chariots. Deborah had to go into battle with Barak since he was haunted by fear, probably a fear of chariots. Nevertheless, God help them win a great victory, and once again the people were set free from oppression. They celebrated in joyful songs.

Challenge

Let's go out today determined not to let the fog of forgetfulness get into our heads, and let us rise up in faith like the Judges, depending on God to deliver us and all those around us.

"Heart Shields Up, Captain"

Proverbs 4

Above all else, guard your heart, for everything you do flows from it. Keep your mouth free of perversity; keep corrupt talk far from your lips. Let your eyes look straight ahead; fix your gaze directly before you. Give careful thought to the paths for your feet and be steadfast in all your ways. Do not turn to the right or the left; keep your foot from evil."

Proverbs 4:23-27 NIV

We've all seen those sci fi movies where the good guys are being attacked. Someone calls out. "Our shields are down to 20%."

Then after more attacks someone says, "10%." When the shields go offline , we know they are doomed. No longer protected, they are prey to the enemy either to be destroyed or boarded. So it is with your heart, if you don't seek God's help in protecting it. If you don't pray or meditate on his word, you are leaving yourself open to attack. You could be taken out before you know it. You could end up like Sampson in Judges 16:20. Though he did not know it, he had become defenseless. The Lord was no longer with him. He presumed that God would always have his back no matter what he did. He had totally let his guard down so that his heart was then far from God. God forbid that we would do the very same thing.

In reality, anyone who doesn't hold tightly to Jesus teaching, is making themselves an easy target for all the dark evil forces in the world, and they may not even be aware of it. (John 8:31-32)

In the end, they could easily, be in the place of the people depicted in Matthew 7:21-23. These people did a lot of great religious things, but they did not really know Jesus, or hold to his teachings. Unfortunately, they were in for a bad eternal surprise that could have and should have been avoided.

Challenge

Let's go out today with our shields up against Satan, and against temptation. If we are feeling especially weak, let's call a friend, and pray for full power to our shield of faith. That way we can stand firm, no matter what comes our way. Then we can help others in need, and share with them the victory and freedom that comes through Christ.

Wisdom vs Folly

Proverbs 9

Which side will you choose?

In this corner, Wisdom waits for you? She's got a really nice house on a solid foundation. She has lots of respectful servants who are sent out to guide you in case you have lost your way. The food at her place is tasty and well prepared.

She wants to share her insight with you.

"Wisdom has built her house; she has set up its seven pillars."

"She has sent out her servants, and she calls from the highest point of the city, "Let all who are simple come to my house!" To those who have no sense she says,"

"Leave your simple ways and you will live; walk in the way of insight."""

Proverbs 9:1, 3-4,6

In this corner, we have Folly, she has decorated herself up to look very appealing, lot's of perfume and make-up. She hangs out near the door of her house where everyone who passes by can see her. She has an affinity for simple-minded folks, hoping to catch their eye. She promises sweet rewards those who taste her delicacies. She calls out to those who want a quick fix for their desires. The only catch is that she is really serving death for dessert. She keeps death deep down in the basement, along with many dead bodies, and conceals the smell with perfume.

“Folly is an unruly woman; she is simple and knows nothing. She sits at the door of her house, on a seat at the highest point of the city, calling out to those who pass by, who go straight on their way,”

““Let all who are simple come to my house!” To those who have no sense she says, “Stolen water is sweet; food eaten in secret is delicious!” But little do they know that the dead are there, that her guests are deep in the realm of the dead.”

Proverbs 9:13-15, 16-18 NIV

To those who escape her grasp, she sends them off on Wideroad turnpike, a well kept but crowded highway. Little do they know, it is a circular road that ends up in her basement, after a while.

Challenge

Let’s go out today determined to steer clear of Folly, or anything that could take us off course. If we are worried about falling off a cliff, would we walk right close to the edge?

No Secrets Allowed

Proverbs 15

Alexa and Suri are listening, and someone is always watching. In today's world, people are concerned about the loss of privacy. With Alexa on the table, and Suri in your pocket, one might forget about the drones peeping in your window, or all the street cams watching your every move. What if someone invented a cam that could see your very thoughts? That would be scary.

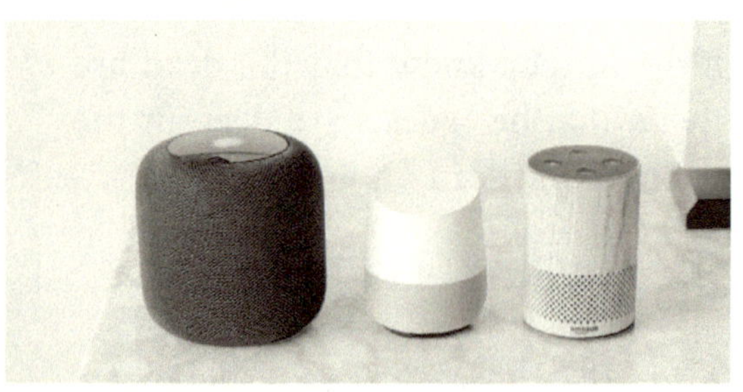

"The eyes of the LORD are everywhere, keeping watch on the wicked and the good."

Proverbs 15:3 NIV

Hold on a minute. He can't do that. We've got our privacy rights. He's not allowed to put eyes everywhere. That would be worse than a stalker.

"Death and Destruction lie open before the LORD — how much more do human hearts!"

Proverbs 15:11 NIV

These eyes not only see us, they even see our heart conditions. And I'm not talking cholesterol, or medical problems. His eyes see far better than 20/20 because they even see death and destruction that we can't see.

Steady as she goes. Set your course straight and upward. Check your GPS, God Positioning System, it's the world's most accurate. Is it going upward or downward? What's it look like up ahead?

"Folly brings joy to one who has no sense, but whoever has understanding keeps a straight course."

Proverbs 15:21 NIV

"The path of life leads upward for the prudent to keep them from going down to the realm of the dead."

Proverbs 15:24 NIV

"The LORD detests the thoughts of the wicked, but gracious words are pure in his sight."

Proverbs 15:26 NIV

Hero to Zero or Zero to Hero, make up your mind.

"Whoever heeds life-giving correction will be at home among the wise. Those who disregard discipline despise themselves, but the one who heeds correction gains understanding. Wisdom's instruction is to fear the LORD, and humility comes before honor."

Proverbs 15:31-33 NIV

Challenge

Let's go out today full of wisdom instead of being full of ourselves. Let's gain some real understanding instead of just money.

Really

Proverbs 16

Mortals make elaborate plans, but GOD has the last word. Humans are satisfied with whatever looks good; GOD probes for what is good. Put GOD in charge of your work, then what you've planned will take place. GOD made everything with a place and purpose; even the wicked are included—but for judgment."

Proverbs 16:1-4 MSG

So, we've got all these plans that sound so cool. We are gonna make all this money. Then we're gonna travel to all these places. We are gonna make everybody happy with our gifts because we are gonna make it happen because we are in charge and nothing's gonna stop us. It's lookin really good to us, but what's the deal, really? Who's runnin this show? Is this real life? Or is it just a show? What happens when the curtain comes down, and the show is over? What happens when, "Looks good," just doesn't hold water anymore?

Challenge

Let's go out today determined to only go after things that make a real difference in this world, and in the next. Otherwise, we will find ourselves chasing after the wind.

Deep Waters

Proverbs 19

"Wine is a mocker and beer a brawler; whoever is led astray by them is not wise."

"It is to one's honor to avoid strife, but every fool is quick to quarrel."

Proverbs 20:1, 3 NIV

"The purposes of a person's heart are deep waters, but one who has insight draws them out."

Proverbs 20:5 NIV

This chapter of Proverbs begins by declaring wine to be a mocker, and beer to be a brawler, and both of them are said to lead people astray.

A mocker is usually someone who makes fun of another through a distasteful, twisted, or exaggerated imitation. It is not a respectful imitation.

The purpose of mocking is usually to make fun of make sport of someone, demeaning their character or appearance, putting them down in some way.

So wine is something the brings down a person's character when they drink too much. It literally turns them into a poor reflection of themselves, not something to be proud of. Wine stands there mocking, calling out, "You're not so great after all. You're just a weak person who needs me to drown your sorrows or to feel happy. On top of that, I make you lose control and follow your craziest impulses. I'm Wine, and I make a mockery out of you."

Beer like wine makes people lose control, and when this happens, anger gets out of control. Brawls are bound to happen. So Beer is really a fight waiting to happen. No wonder the writer says here that Beer and Wine lead people astray. Kinda like these two things that put us on a leash and drag us off.

Challenge

Let's go out today determined not to let anything drag us off. Once addiction takes hold, it's gonna take a lot to get us free.

"To the Jews who had believed him, Jesus said, "If you hold to my teaching, you are really my disciples. Then you will know the truth, and the truth will set you free.""

John 8:31-32 NIV

Woe is Me, So is Me

Psalm 17

Woe is me, so is me.

"A cheerful disposition is good for your health; gloom and doom leave you bone-tired."

Proverbs 17:22 MSG

There's a reason people say, "I'm sick and tired of .... whatever. When we begin to make negative predictions, we are starting what people call, "self fulfilling prophecies." We appoint ourselves a prophet despite having no knowledge of the future and we predict the worst possible outcome. Then we burn all our energy worrying about it and damaging our health.

Why not just trust God to deal with the future because he is the only one who knows it. Since he already sees the outcome, there's no need for us to burn ourselves out worrying about it.

The only thing we should be worrying about is what will happen to us, if we reject the directions that God is trying to give us through his word and through Godly people he has placed in our lives. If we think, we know better than he who holds the future in his hands, then we are headed for trouble.

Challenge

Let's not go out today, before we check in with God through prayer and Bible study. After that, we can check in with godly friends who will help us to stay on track. Then we can be sure that we are on the path to victory, no matter what obstacles we may be facing.

Who's Our Landlord?

Psalm 24

Is it the guy we pay money to every month? No. Is it the government we pay taxes to? Is it the State we live in who makes a lot of rules to follow?

Is it the dr who tries to keep us healthy? Nope, it's not any of these. The landlord is the guy who owns the place. In our case, it is also the guy who made the place. For a time, he had given us a place to live.

"......he himself gives everyone life and breath and everything else. From one man he made all the nations, that they should inhabit the whole earth; and he marked out their appointed times in history and the boundaries of their lands. God did this so that they would seek him and perhaps reach out for him and find him, though he is not far from any one of us."

Acts 17:25-27

He has given us bodies to live in. If we abuse these bodies, we could easily get kicked out early before our time is up.

"The earth is the Lord's, and everything in it, the world, and all who live in it;"

Psalms 24:1 NIV

Unlike a worldly landlord, our heavenly landlord actually wants to get to know us. If we take the time to get to know him, he will even grant us a lot of comfort and benefits.

Who is our heavenly Landlord? We're in luck because it's also our heavenly Dad. In fact, our Dad owns everything we can see. How cool is that?

But as we can see on the news, the world is a mess. There is all kinds of garbage going on and even an evil virus stalking us, one at a time.

On top of all of that, there is a virus that we already caught called sin and it can be quite deadly. "for all have sinned and fall short of the glory of God," "For the wages of sin is death,…"

Romans 3:23; 6:23

There is only one cure for it and it's very expensive. It cost the very life of our own Landlord's Son to make it available to us. Yet, most people don't even bother to look for it. Our Landlord has even given out free testing kits to everyone. "Examine yourselves to see whether you are in the faith; test yourselves. Do you not realize that Christ Jesus is in you—unless, of course, you fail the test?"

2 Corinthians 13:5

Most of us already have one in our home, it's called the Bible. But like with any test kit, we've got to know how to use it, and for that we've got to find a faithful disciple to help us out.

Challenge

Let's go out today determined to be thankful for all that our Heavenly Landlord has done for us. Because if we remain faithful to him, he has promised us a heavenly retirement home with him that will never be shut down.

Chosen, But You Must Choose

Amos 3, 4

"You only have I chosen of all

the families of the earth; therefore I will punish you for all your sins." Amos 3:2 NIV

When you are chosen for something, it usually results in a positive feeling.

Maybe you were chosen to be on a team, or chosen to get into a great college. This would be a cause for celebration. What if God, were to come to you and say, I'm choosing you to be my special friend, part of my family? That's how Amos 3 begins. Then he says because I have chosen you, I am going to punish you.

We live in an age where cheap grace reigns, and no strings attached Christianity is the rule, where undisciplined children grow into undisciplined adults. But the Bible speaks of discipline as being an expression of love.

"Those whom I love I rebuke and discipline. So be earnest and repent."

Revelation 3:19 NIV

"Endure hardship as discipline; God is treating you as his children. For what children are not disciplined by their father? If you are not disciplined—and everyone undergoes discipline—then you are not legitimate, not true sons and daughters at all."

Hebrews 12:7-8 NIV

God expects his people to return to him after they are punished.

““I overthrew some of you as I overthrew Sodom and Gomorrah. You were like a burning stick snatched from the fire, yet you have not returned to me,” declares the LORD.”

Amos 4:11 NIV

Even those who do not return are ultimately called to face him like a criminal arrested and brought before a judge.

““Therefore this is what I will do to you, Israel, and because I will do this to you, Israel, prepare to meet your God.””

Amos 4:12 NIV

It is much better to come voluntarily and develop a loving relationship with God through his word, than to be dragged before him because we have rejected him.

“For he has set a day when he will judge the world with justice by the man he has appointed. He has given proof of this to everyone by raising him from the dead.””

Acts 17:31 NIV

Challenge

Let’s go out today remembering that it is ultimately up to us whether to choose a loving relationship with our heavenly Father now, or a not so good relationship with our heavenly Judge later.

Come On.

Isaiah 65

All day long I have held out my hands to an obstinate people, who walk in ways not good, pursuing their own imaginations—"

Isaiah 65:2 NIV

"..........for I called but you did not answer, I spoke but you did not listen. You did evil in my sight and chose what displeases me.""

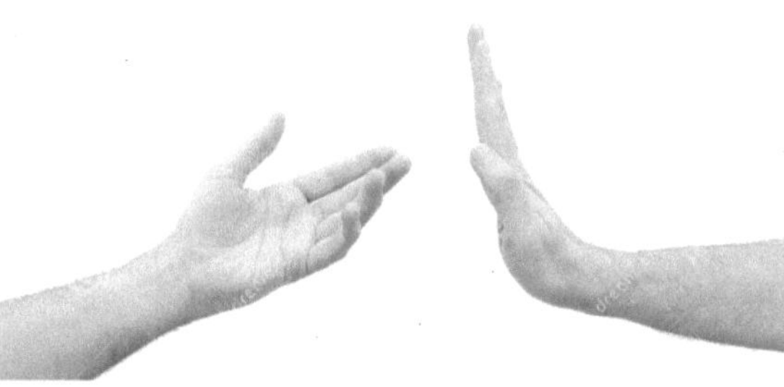

Isaiah 65:12 NIV

"Where's your homework?" calls out the teacher after checking the papers on her desk. This is usually followed by a flood of excuses as to why it wasn't done. Bottom line is, most of the students either forgot to do it, or just didn't listen when it was assigned and spent their day doing as they pleased.

While God, is far more important than a teacher, he, like a teacher, has expectations. He expects us not to follow our own imaginations, and do whatever we feel like doing. If we do this, there will be some serious consequences, far worse than a few bad grades.

God speaks to our very heart and soul. He cares for us and longs for us. He longs for a great relationship with us because he created us and knows how we should behave correctly. He holds out his hands to us all day long like we are wandering lost children. Have you talked with your heavenly father today? He is waiting.

Challenge

Let's go out today, determined to keep in touch with our God as much as possible. When we finally arrive at the Pearly Gates, we want to hear, "It's great to see you," not "Who are you? I don't know you."

The Great Custody Battle Pt 1

We're here outside the JSC Courthouse reporting on the well known custody battle between the Heavenly Father and the Devil, himself. The children, also known as, the souls of men, are being held by Family Services awaiting the outcome of the trial.

We are among a throng of reporters waiting, just outside, for the proceedings to begin. Wait! We've just been told that the Heavenly Father is arriving with his entourage nearby. Let's see if we can get a statement on his way in. Over here, in the parking area, we can see several cars pulling up, including a large white SUV labeled Tesla Cloud, that's the new 2021 electric model.

The Heavenly Father is coming out out and starting his way into the court. Let's see if we can get a brief statement.

Heavenly Father, can you give a brief statement about your intentions regarding this custody hearing for the souls of men. He pauses for a moment and then replies, "As I have said before, "I will live with them and walk among them, and I will be their God, and they will be my people." "I will be a Father to" them, "and" they "will be my sons and daughters, says the Lord Almighty."

2 Corinthians 6:16, 18

Thank you Heavenly Father, and good luck in court today. You can see the Heavenly Father making his way into the courthouse, while we wait outside for the opposition.

Suddenly, we can see in the parking area several dark red vehicles approaching looking like flashy sports cars. They park in the no parking area and several scantily clad women quickly get out and open the door for the Devil, himself. They escort him down the walkway and are headed this way. Let's see if we can get a statement. Sir, Mr Devil, Sir, would your care to make a statement for our viewers?

"Of course, young man, I'll tell you this. All those nasty things, you've heard about me are not true. I've been blamed for a lot things that are not my fault. I've been victimized by a lot of folks trying to pin stuff on me that is really their own fault. We all got freedom to choose. These kids have chosen me to be their father by their own actions, and nobody's gonna take them away from me. Together, we've had so much fun, at least we did for awhile.

Thank you for your statement Sir. "And one more thing," said the Devil, interrupting.

"Those people who said all those things about me. They better watch their backs. As far as I'm concerned, they can go to hell along with their friends. And tell that parking guy to leave my cars alone too."

Okay, folks, that's all for now. We'll be following this case closely, as it proceeds in court. This is your Ace reporter signing off.

To be Continued

Challenge

Let's go out today remembering that our Heavenly Father will fight to keep us safe and close to his heart.

The Great Custody Battle

(Continued)

Good evening, Ladies and Gentlemen, this is your Ace reporter here, once again, waiting outside of the JSC Courthouse. We understand that this case has taken quite some time and has had many twists and turns.

For instance, the Devil was accused of attempting to bribe the judge. Matthew 4:3. But the judge turned him down. Right after that, he caused a conspiracy and tried to have the judge taken out. Luke 22:3

There appeared to be no end to the stunts the Devil would attempt to try to win his case for the Souls of Men. He tried everything from lying to the court (John 8:44) under an oath which he took over a fake Bible which was really a comic book.

In the end, he had to be bound with chains, and held for the Judges final decision.

"He seized the dragon, that ancient serpent, who is the devil, or Satan, and bound

him …."

Revelation 20:2 NIV

Okay, I believe, there's about to be a verdict announcement passed out to the press. It looks like multiple verdicts since there are several envelopes.

Okay, here's the first one, it reads. "Unfortunately, Mr. Ima Devil has been taken into custody and has been scheduled to be cast on into the lake of fire along with all of his co-conspirators at a designated time. For now, he has been released on bail.

Regarding the Souls of Men: Despite great attempts by the Heavenly Father to adopt all of them, many of them have shown a strong desire to stay with their step father. So, it is the decision of this court that anyone whose name is not written in the Heavenly Father's book shall be allowed to accompany their step father wherever he might be." "This is the verdict: Light has come into the world, but people loved darkness instead of light because their deeds were evil."

John 3:19 NIV

"Anyone whose name was not found written in the book of life was thrown into the lake of fire."

Revelation 20:15

Concerning those whose names are written in the Heavenly Father's book, they will receive their official adoption papers and accompany him back to his very large mansion where there will stay forever.

"And I heard a loud voice from the throne saying, "Look! God's dwelling place is now among the people, and he will dwell with them. They will be his people, and God himself will be with them and be their God. 'He will wipe every tear from their eyes. ..."

Revelation 21:3-4 NIV

Challenge

Let's go out today determined to get our names in the Heavenly Father's book, and help many others to get their names in the book as well. "I tell you, now is the time of God's favor, now is the day of salvation."

2 Corinthians 6:2 NIV

Comfort is More than Food

2 Corinthians 1

We all love our comfort foods, but can they really give us the comfort we need, or will they just make us comfortable in our current mess, and not really relieve our distress.

"Praise be to the God and Father of our Lord Jesus Christ, the Father of compassion and the God of all comfort, who comforts us in all our troubles, so that we can comfort those in any trouble with the comfort we ourselves receive from God."

2 Corinthians 1:3-4

If you're in need of real comfort, you might as well get it from the God of all comfort. Comforting is one of the things that God does best. Nobody does it better. If we got trouble, God has the comfort that can get us through it. Food is just not gonna do it.

In fact, God's comfort is so awesome that we can pass it on to our friends, and this can help them in their own troubles.

"For just as we share abundantly in the sufferings of Christ, so also our comfort abounds through Christ. If we are distressed, it is for your comfort and salvation; if we are comforted, it is for your comfort, which produces in you patient endurance of the same sufferings we suffer. And our hope for you is firm, because we know that just as you share in our sufferings, so also you share in our comfort."

2 Corinthians 1:5-7

If we are suffering, in need of patient endurance. We better stock up on comfort, because we're gonna need it. If we've got the right kind of comfort, we can endure anything.

We could turn to our comfort friends, our comfort movies, or even our comfort sins, but the best comfort will always come from our comforting God.

"We do not want you to be uninformed, brothers and sisters, about the troubles we experienced .... We were under great pressure, far beyond our ability to endure, so that we despaired of life itself. Indeed, we felt we had received the sentence of death. But this happened that we might not rely on ourselves but on God, who raises the dead."

2 Corinthians 1:8-9

Challenge

Let's go out today remembering that when the pressures of life start to get to us, we have a God that we can rely on who is "the God of all comfort."

Written On My Heart

2 Corinthians 3

What's on your heart this morning. Like a Valentines card, there's something special about things written on a heart. Our hearts are tablets and are really designed to be written on by God and his people. It's there for people to read, not to be covered up, or erased. Are we being open about our heats today, or hiding them in our closets, afraid to let others see who we really are on the inside? Have we let our heart be full of pollution and obscenities? Are we afraid to let anyone see what's on our heart.

"Are we beginning to commend ourselves again? Or do we need, like some people, letters of recommendation to you or from you? You yourselves are our letter, written on our hearts, known and read by everyone. You show that you are a letter from Christ, the result of our ministry, written not with ink but with the Spirit of the living God, not on tablets of stone but on tablets of human hearts."

2 Corinthians 3:1-3

Maybe we've let our heart become so polluted by the world that God can't write on them anymore. Our hearts are literally turning to stone. We feel like we can't feel any deep feelings at all any more. All we can feel is pain. In that case, it's time for a spiritual heart transplant, or maybe a pace maker to restore our hearts to life again.

Like it or not, to some extent, our hearts are supposed to be "known and read by everyone."

Since we are often given to fear, selfishness, and sin, it's easy to, like many, let our hearts be covered up thus we become self deceived and a veil covers our hearts. We just can't seem to see straight anymore.

The Jews in Paul's day had a similar problem.

"Even to this day when Moses is read, a veil covers their hearts. But whenever anyone turns to the Lord, the veil is taken away."

2 Corinthians 3:15-16

The answer is simple. We must turn to the Lord. He will take care of our hearts and make them new regardless of their condition.

"I will sprinkle clean water on you, and you will be clean; I will cleanse you from all your impurities and from all your idols. I will give you a new heart and put a new spirit in you; I will remove from you your heart of stone and give you a heart of flesh. And I will put my Spirit in you and move you to follow my decrees and be careful to keep my laws." Ezek 36:25-27

Challenge

Today, let's go out with a new heart devoted to doing all the awesome things that God has planned for us. That way we can share not only our faith but our hearts as well.

Like the song by One Plus in the early 2000s says, "You, you're in my soul wherever I go

Now I know right from the start,
Your love was written on my heart."

Today, let's give our hearts to God who is a real heart specialist because he designed our hearts to match up with his. Without him, a piece of our heart will always be missing.

Someone Turn the Light On!

2 Corinthians 4

A few years ago, the movie Tangled came out about a girl who grew up, not knowing who she really was and what to do with her life. She couldn't see much from the tower room where she lived, until later in the story when her eyes were opened. Much like us, we are born into this world, not really knowing what we are doing here. We need someone to shed some light on our situation.

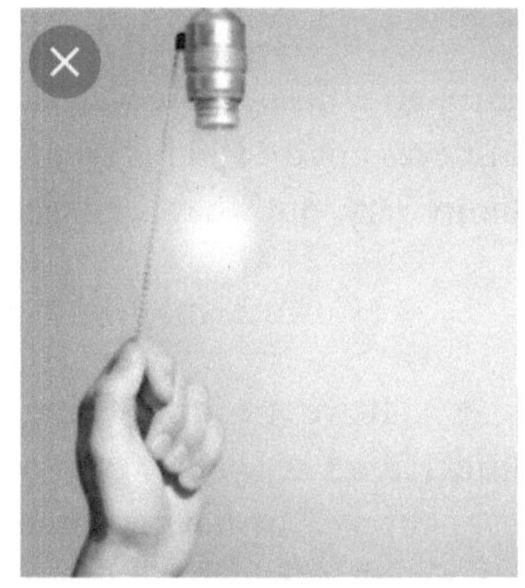

"And even if our gospel (good news) is veiled, it is veiled to those who are perishing. The god of this age has blinded the minds of unbelievers, so that they cannot see the light of the gospel that displays the glory of Christ, who is the image of God."

2 Corinthians 4:3-4

In the movie, the evil Gothel had blinded Rapunzel by keeping the good news of who she really was hidden away from her.

"For God, who said, "Let light shine out of darkness," made his light shine in our hearts to give us the light of the knowledge of God's glory displayed in the face of Christ."

2 Corinthians 4:6 NIV

In this case, God shines the light, right passed the eyes and into the heart. Talk about a penetrating light, way stronger than even the sun or a laser. And what kind of vision does it give us, when are eyes are opened again? Why, we can even sense things that were invisible before. We know that anything we have to endure will soon be over.

"For our light and momentary troubles are achieving for us an eternal glory that far outweighs them all."

2 Corinthians 4:17 NIV

Our vision can be even better than superman's who can see through walls because we've chosen to have a different focus. "So we fix our eyes not on what is seen, but on what is unseen, since what is seen is temporary, but what is unseen is eternal."

2 Corinthians 4:18

If we are still feeling lost in a fog, perhaps we've never really understood how good the good news really is. We need to go have our eyes checked by having some really great eye opening Bible studies and talks with friends. Then we can have a deeper understanding of the following lyric:

"All those days watching from the windows

All those years outside looking in.

All that time never even knowing

Just how blind I've been.

Now I'm here blinking in the starlight.

Now I'm here suddenly I see,

Standing here, it's all so clear

I'm where I'm meant to be,

And at last I see the light,

And it's like the fog has lifted,

And at last I see the light,

And it's like the sky is new,

And it's warm and real and bright,

And the world has somehow shifted.

All at once everything looks different,

Now that I see you."

Challenge

Let's go out today with our eyes fixed on what really matters, so that our lives can really make a difference. Then we can really be who we were meant to be.

"Battle Stations"

Ephesians 6

Battle! Stations," is the call to prepare for an imminent conflict, but this time it's not the Klingons, the Borg, or even Darth Vadar. It's something far worse, and we better be ready for the day of evil because it's coming whether we are expecting it on not.

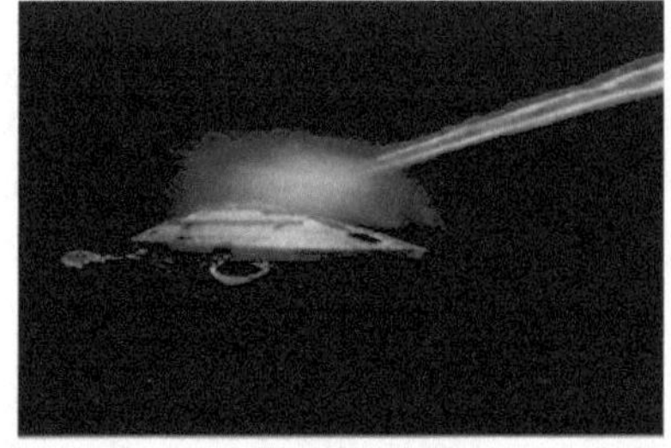

Shields at 20% and holding!

"For our struggle is not against flesh and blood, but against the rulers, against the authorities, against the powers of this dark world and against the spiritual forces of evil in the heavenly realms. Therefore put on the full armor of God, so that when the day of evil comes, you may be able to stand your ground, and after you have done everything, to stand."

Ephesians 6:12-13

The battle is on and our enemy knows all the tricks in the book, and will stop at nothing to win.

"Put on the full armor of God, so that you can take your stand against the devil's schemes."

Ephesians 6:11 NIV

Believe it or not, right now, the devil is scheming on how he's gonna take us down. He's got plans A, B, C, and D, all set to go, and more if that doesn't work. So, we'd better be ready with our 🛡 shield of faith. If we don't have one, we better start with Romans 10:17 and get one. Otherwise, we're done, all but the funeral. It's time to get our armor on. Without it, we are sitting ducks, easy to pick off. If we've got any friends, we'd better help them with their armor. If they are fence sitters with little conviction, they will be the first on Satan's hit list. Church going will never replace God's armor, so that alone just won't hack it. We will be looking like a porcupine full of Satan's darts.

Challenge

Let's go out today with our full armor on knowing that we are saved, with our feet ready to go and share the good news, fully grounded in the truth about our lives and relationship with God and others, ready to use the word of God as our sword bashing on the powers of Satan to set others free from the forces of darkness.

Let us us quickly get to our battle stations because we are taking it to the enemy. We are ready to light up the world.

The Way of Suffering, the Path of Glory

Philippians 1

The package is late again, that guy cut us off in traffic. That lady in line keeps arguing with the cashier, backing up the only register open in the store. We can't find any person in the hardware store who can tell us where the hammers are. If it takes longer, we are going to beat them with a hammer.

This is the modern path of suffering. When the ice cream machine breaks down at McDonalds again, we just go off the rails. We have little understanding of the true path of suffering until we are faced with a pandemic as we are today. In Philippians, Paul unveils to us a unique kind of suffering which is purely voluntary, but absolutely essential to anyone seeking to be a disciple of Jesus.

"In your relationships with one another, have the same mindset as Christ Jesus: Who, being in very nature God, did not consider equality with God something to be used to his own advantage; rather, he made himself nothing by taking the very nature of a servant, being made in human likeness. And being found in appearance as a man, he humbled himself by becoming obedient to death— even death on a cross!"

Philippians 2:5-8 NIV

These verses are absolutely amazing describing the absolute humility of Jesus, "who made himself nothing," compared to "being in very nature God." Who of us are are ready to volunteer to become a lowly nothing servant for the benefit of someone else? The pay is below minimum wage, and at the end of the day, you're going to be beaten, and brutally murdered on a cross. Who wants to volunteer? Jesus raised his hand because he loves us. He knew that in his loss, he would achieve victory for us, and anyone who would choose to follow him.

We all want to be exalted, but the mistake we make is that we exalt ourselves, or seek to be exalted by other people. It bothers us, when people don't notice our efforts or compliment out work.

We've got it all wrong because true life is not about us, it's about helping others and seeking to please God. If we do this then God himself will exalt us, even if nobody else notices. Look what he did for Jesus.

"Therefore God exalted him to the highest place and gave him the name that is above every name, that at the name of Jesus every knee should bow, in heaven and on earth and under the earth, and every tongue acknowledge that Jesus Christ is Lord, to the glory of God the Father."

Philippians 2:9-11 NIV

Challenge

Let's go out today and make ourselves nothing servants to love and care for others because we follow someone by the name of Jesus, who did the same for us. Then whatever sufferings we endure will be an honor because we will get to share just a bit in the sufferings of our Lord.

Will we truly answer Jesus when he calls, "Come follow me."

Who of us is willing to stand up and call out boldly, "Yes, Lord, I'm coming? Wait up."

For me to live is What?

Colossians 3, Philippians 1

Everyday, most of us go to work, or we do our household chores, feed the kids, and the pets, pay the bills, fix whatever is broken, do the shopping, watch our favorite shows, check on the relatives, do the laundry, and then go to bed. Then we wake up and do it all over again except for an occasional fun outing for a break. We may even check out a church service once and awhile, if we're feeling guilty about any misdeeds we may have done. What are our hearts and minds focused on? What are we living for?

"Since, then, you have been raised with Christ, set your hearts on things above, where Christ is, seated at the right hand of God. Set your minds on things above, not on earthly things."

Colossians 3:1-2

Paul says that if we are disciples, our hearts and minds now have a different focus than most folks. Our hearts are set on things above, and our minds where Christ is seated, and our minds are also set on things above too.

If this isn't the case, then we are headed off course. Our God Positioning System (GPS)is not set. Instead, we have let the world set our course, and our focus is now on us, and how much comfort or pleasure we can get in this world. At some point, we will have to check our hearts, hopefully before the check engine light comes on for our lives. By then, it may be too late.

"When Christ, who is your life, appears, then you also will appear with him in glory.

Let the message of Christ dwell among you richly as you teach and admonish one another with all wisdom through psalms, hymns, and songs from the Spirit, singing to God with gratitude in your hearts. And whatever you do, whether in word or deed, do it all in the name of the Lord Jesus, giving thanks to God the Father through him."

Colossians 3:4, 16-17

Is the message of Christ dwelling in us richly? Are we teaching and admonishing others to be closer to God. Are we singing songs of thankfulness throughout our days.

Are we doing everything we do in the name of the Lord, or are we just doing our own thing, seeking the approval of people rather than God? Can we echoe what Paul said near the end of his life, "For to me, to live is Christ and to die is gain."

Philippians 1:21 NIV

Challenge

Let's go out today, remembering that, if we are true disciples, for us to live is Christ, for Christ is our life. If our life is something else, it's time to open the Bible for a real heart and mind check.

Steady as She Goes

1 Timothy

Paul left Timothy in Ephesus to guide the disciples through the storms of life. Some had changed their course and made a shipwreck of their faith. They thought they knew a better way, or perhaps a shortcut. But they didn't know their lives would end up on one of Satan's sandbars, or hidden reefs.

"holding on to faith and a good conscience, which some have rejected and so have suffered shipwreck with regard to the faith."

1 Timothy 1:19 NIV

Others have simply jumped ship and wandered off on their own. When faithful disciples looked for them, they couldn't be found. They were trapped by the old "grass is greener on the other side" trick that Satan used to get them off the ship.

"The Spirit clearly says that in later times some will abandon the faith and follow deceiving spirits and things taught by demons."

1 Timothy 4:1 NIV

If we've jumped ship, it doesn't matter how nice looking we are, we are still going to drown eventually. If we are in a lifeboat, it will have cracks, and the life will leak out if it.

"For the love of money is a root of all kinds of evil. Some people, eager for money, have wandered from the faith and pierced themselves with many griefs."

1 Timothy 6:10

"Turn away from godless chatter and the opposing ideas of what is falsely called knowledge, which some have professed and in so doing have departed from the faith."

1 Timothy 6:20-21 NIV

Wandering on our own in search of $

Challenge

Today, before we go out, let's remember that God is able to get us through whatever storm we are facing. We don't have to abandon our faith, our clear conscience, our walk with God. If we stay on board with him, he will guide us to a peaceful and safe harbor, so let us hold on tight.

The Path to Leadership

1 Timothy 3

Lots of people would like to be leaders. The pay is better, and how about the prestige. People look up to you, and say nice things about you. But it's that really what godly leadership is about.

Paul gives us a lot of clues in this chapter. It's not so much seeking the leadership position that is important but being the right person that is important. A true leader will be leading long before anyone recognizes him.

"Here is a trustworthy saying: Whoever aspires to be an overseer desires a noble task."

1 Timothy 3:1 NIV

Godly leading is a noble task requiring a noble person. If we are ignoble, and irresponsible, then we are certainly not destined for godly leadership. Let's look at the checklist that Paul gives us for qualities of a great leader.

"Now the overseer is to be above reproach, faithful to his wife, temperate, self-controlled, respectable, hospitable, able to teach, not given to drunkenness, not violent but gentle, not quarrelsome, not a lover of money. He must manage his own family well and see that his children obey him, and he must do so in a manner worthy of full respect. (If anyone does not know how to manage his own family, how can he take care of God's church?)"

1 Timothy 3:2-5 NIV

So, before we jump into leadership, we must ask ourselves a few questions. Do we love serving? A true leader will serve with or without recognition. A true leader will rise up to leadership, not be arbitrarily placed in leadership because of academic status, or worldly accomplishments. A true leader will raise up others to lead along with him.

Challenge

As we go out today, lets remember that Jesus came to serve, not to be served. If we have this heart of humble service, then we are headed toward the true path of leadership. Who are we going to serve today?

Death Destroyed

2 Timothy 1

But it has now been revealed through the appearing of our Savior, Christ Jesus, who has destroyed death and has brought life and immortality to light through the gospel."

2 Timothy 1:10

There have been millions of tombstones over the centuries, but thanks to Jesus, death itself has now been given one. While it may not seem like it, but death's days are now numbered. It's power is now beginning to fade.

"But God raised him from the dead, freeing him from the agony of death, because it was impossible for death to keep its hold on him."

Acts 2:24 NIV

There we have it, death starting to lose it's grip. It may not sound like much, one out of billions raising from the dead. But like a small crack in a dam, it's only a matter of time before a flood begins. Life and immortality are starting to come to light.

But this new life and immortality will only be made available to those who have entrusted themselves to God, as Paul had.

"That is why I am suffering as I am. Yet this is no cause for shame, because I know whom I have believed, and am convinced that he is able to guard what I have entrusted to him until that day."

2 Timothy 1:12 NIV

What are we trusting in today, our talents, our bank accounts, our family and friends? None of these have the power for us to rise from the dead. They can make us feel good for awhile, but all that is temporary. The word clearly says that we can't even trust ourselves. "This is what the Lord says: "Cursed is the one who trusts in man, who draws strength from mere flesh and whose heart turns away from the Lord."

Jeremiah 17:5 NIV

If we put our trust in anyone but the Lord, our hearts will turn away and we will be cursed instead of blessed. We will lose our chance to take hold of eternal life, like a butterfly, it will slip through our fingers, because we did not entrust our lives to God.

Challenge

Let's go out today, remembering to rely on God, and not ourselves. We do not know the way on our own. We need to always follow our guide. "Jesus answered, "I am the way and the truth and the life. No one comes to the Father except through me."

John 14:6 NIV

Missing in Action

2 Timothy 2-3

"The War isn't over till the last soldier comes home." This was the theme of the Chuck Norris rescue movie of the early 1980s. He was not about to forget his comrades who were still being held as captives. Being an ex-prisoner himself, he knew what it was like to be held captive, and tortured far from home, and freedom.

"Opponents must be gently instructed, in the hope that God will grant them repentance leading them to a knowledge of the truth, and that they will come to their senses and escape from the trap of the devil, who has taken them captive to do his will."

2 Timothy 2:25-26

Today, we face a different yet far more dangerous enemy who is an expert at hand to hand combat. His prisoners are then sent out like child soldiers in combat to do his will. They have lost their freewill even if they don't know it. They are now on the side of darkness and the desires of the flesh. They fight against the forces of goodness and light. They make fun of those who stand up for righteousness and godly values like Bible studies. Or perhaps, they might be holding to a form of godliness, but denying it's power.

"People will be lovers of themselves, lovers of money, boastful, proud, abusive, disobedient to their parents, ungrateful, unholy, without love, unforgiving, slanderous, without self-control, brutal, not lovers of the good, treacherous, rash, conceited, lovers of pleasure rather than lovers of God— having a form of godliness but denying its power. Have nothing to do with such people."

2 Timothy 3:2-5 NIV

Regardless of what role they are playing, they are still under the power of the evil one, and they are in need of being rescued.

The work of rescuers is hard, and sometimes rewarded by a slap in the face.

"In fact, everyone who wants to live a godly life in Christ Jesus will be persecuted,"

2 Timothy 3:12 NIV

But like the rescuers when the Miami condo fell last year, we will not give up. As long as there's a chance that someone may respond, we will call out to them with the good news that they can be saved and set free. "To the Jews who had believed him, Jesus said, "If you hold to my teaching, you are really my disciples. Then you will know the truth, and the truth will set you free.""

John 8:31-32 NIV

Challenge

Let's go out today remembering Jesus' call to freedom, if we would but hold to his teaching. We have his teaching in the Bible, the very road map to freedom. Let's go out and share it with people, and then watch many of the captive souls in the world being set free.

Out of Nowhere, Kindness Appeared

Titus 3

At one time we too were foolish, disobedient, deceived and enslaved by all kinds of passions and pleasures."

Titus 3:3 NIV

"But when the kindness and love of God our Savior appeared, he saved us, not because of righteous things we had done, but because of his mercy. He saved us through the washing of rebirth and renewal by the Holy Spirit, whom he poured out on us generously through Jesus Christ our Savior,"

Titus 3:4-6 NIV

Ever been caught red handed, like with our hands and feet in the cookie jar. We are like a bank robber who left his wallet at the scene of the crime, or a car thief who got himself locked in the car he was trying to steal. God has us red handed and red faced.

We were "foolish, disobedient, deceived and enslaved by all kinds of passions and pleasures." We were in pretty bad shape and most of us didn't even realize how bad off we were because we were Deceived with a capital D. We thought we were free, but we were really enslaved by our own passions and desires of all kinds. We were really in need of kindness and mercy to get us out of our slavery.

We really needed a fresh start, a clean slate, a washing of rebirth, not just a car wash. We also needed a new source of power to keep us on the right track. This power comes only through the Holy Spirit, and the clean slate comes only through the working of God at baptism. Colossians 2:12. Acts 2:38

Challenge

Let's go out today remembering that if we have been reborn, we are now heirs to a new life. We have now been adopted by the most powerful being in the universe, and given the hope of eternal life, way better than winning the lottery. Our prize already given to us is a new life that will never end. If we have been reborn, the graveyard no longer marks the end for us, but simply our promotion to the home office.

"Hello, who's this?"

Hebrews 1

"This is the creator of the universe speaking. Who's this?"

How do we answer a call from the creator of the universe? Do we pay attention, tor do we write it off as a prank call. Or, do we hang up because we believe that we are too insignificant for him to be calling us, or because we are just flat out too sinful and would rather not speak to someone who knows all the bad stuff we have done, and all of the ways we have messed up our lives. Or we might just be afraid that he is calling to end our lives or to put a stop to all of our fun.

Before we hang up, we might just want to listen to see if he has any good news for us that might get us out of our bad situations we find ourselves in.

"In the past God spoke to our ancestors through the prophets at many times and in various ways, but in these last days he has spoken to us by his Son, whom he appointed heir of all things, and through whom also he made the universe. The Son is the radiance of God's glory and the exact representation of his being, sustaining all things by his powerful word. After he had provided purification for sins, he sat down at the right hand of the Majesty in heaven."

Hebrews 1:1-3 NIV

There's an old song entitled, "Jesus is Calling." Well, that song may be truer than we think. But before we shy away saying, "How did he get my number?" we must remember that since he made everything, he has always had our number. He knows us even better than we know ourselves. So if he's calling, we'd better be answering.

Challenge

Let's go out today remembering that he's got some good news for us, if we would just be willing to listen and follow his direction. He will send us on the best course in life with his God Positioning System.

The Cure for Death

Hebrews 2

Today, we face a worldwide plague that has filled the hospitals, as well as the funeral homes. Despite vaccine progress, the Corona virus continues to stalk our streets and homes looking for an opening.

Doctors work day and night searching for a cure.

All the while, a far more deadlier plague also works its way though unsuspecting homes. That is the plague of death. Often depicted as a skeleton in a robe with a sickle in his hands, he makes his way into the rooms of the elderly, as well as the alleys of violent neighborhoods and crowded freeways.

This death is in reality an agent of Satan himself. Satan knows that in death, he hurts the God who loves all of the souls of men. In the midst of this devastation, one man rose up against death itself to provide a way of escape for all God's lost children, including us.

"Since the children have flesh and blood, Jesus too shared in their humanity so that by his death he might break the power of him who holds the power of death—that is, the devil— and free those who all their lives were held in slavery by their fear of death."

Hebrews 2:14-15 NIV

To break this chain of suffering, Jesus had to endure everything that we might endure, every obstacle that we might face.

"For this reason he had to be made like them, fully human in every way, in order that he might become a merciful and faithful high priest in service to God, and that he might make atonement for the sins of the people. Because he himself suffered when he was tempted, he is able to help those who are being tempted."

Hebrews 2:17-18 NIV

Challenge

Let's go out today remembering that Jesus has faced anything that we might face, yet he was able to overcome. Also, he provides a way for us to overcome all of our mistakes and slip-ups, if we would but hold to his teaching. Freedom from both sin and death can come to us with every sunrise.

"To the Jews who had believed him, Jesus said, "If you hold to my teaching, you are really my disciples. Then you will know the truth, and the truth will set you free.""

John 8:31-32 NIV

The Taste of Death

Hebrews 2

We are the Kings of a fictional kingdom called, "Do Your Own Thing." We have many subjects, but we pay little attention to them, since we care little for anyone. We enjoy traveling around our kingdom to see how much better off we are than all the peasantry. We lie to them with many false promises telling them that we care for them. Because of our harshness, we have many enemies, so we have to hire a food taster just in case someone tries to poison us, as well as body guards to protect us and to give us compliments. Inside, we feel bad about all that we have done, but these compliments make us feel better and cover our misdeeds.

One day, our food taster is tasting a nice looking meal when suddenly, he grabs his throat, falls over and dies. We are deeply disturbed, not because of his friendship and sacrifice, but because we will have to go out and find another food taster willing to risk his life. It is gonna cost us more money this time.

"But we do see Jesus, who was made lower than the angels for a little while, now crowned with glory and honor because he suffered death, so that by the grace of God he might taste death for everyone."

Hebrews 2:9 NIV

We have heard ever since we were children that Jesus died for the world and that Jesus loves us for the Bible tells us so. But it doesn't mean much until we until we understand that Jesus took on something that was meant for us. Not only that, but it was our own sinful wicked deeds that put him on that cross.

"This man was handed over to you by God's deliberate plan and foreknowledge; and you, with the help of wicked men, put him to death by nailing him to the cross."

Acts 2:23 NIV

"..... the Lord Jesus Christ, who gave himself for our sins to rescue us from the present evil age, according to the will of our God and Father,"

Galatians 1:3-4 NIV

So, Jesus literally took our place. We deserved to be on that cross for our sin. That cross had our name on it, just as surely as that food in the story was intended for us. Are we just going to walk away like it was no big deal, while in reality, it was the biggest deal ever?

Challenge

Let's go out today, determined to be grateful for all that has been done for us, remembering that someone cared enough to taste death for us because he loved us so much.

Tug of War

Hebrews 3

How many of us have ever been involved in a tug of war contest? First you size up the opposing team. If there's a big guy at the other end of the rope, you know it's gonna be tough.

So it begins. The rope goes back and forth. Some people drop the rope. You scream at them, "Just hold on tight." Eventually the team that holds on tightest and pulls the hardest wins among the cheers.

In Hebrews 3, the writer issues the same call to hold on. In this case the stakes are much higher than a game. In this case the losers lose their very soul.

"But Christ is faithful as the Son over God's house. And we are his house, if indeed we hold firmly to our confidence and the hope in which we glory."

Hebrews 3:6 NIV

"We have come to share in Christ, if indeed we hold our original conviction firmly to the very end."

Hebrews 3:14 NIV

Just as in a tug of war contest where many fall down and some even give up, this contest requires perseverance, character, and determination. These contestants must believe that God is with them and must have faith to give it their whole heart.

"Now the promise of entering into God's rest is still for us today. So we must be extremely careful to ensure that we all embrace the fullness of that promise and not fail to experience it. For we have heard the good news of deliverance just as they did, yet they didn't join their faith with the Word. Instead, what they heard didn't affect them deeply, for they doubted."

Hebrews 4:1-2 TPT

Challenge

Lets go out today remembering to hold on tight to our confidence, our conviction, and our faith prompted by love.

If we loose our grip, we will be pulled into darkness and eventually give up all together.

Get At Peace With God Now, or There will be No Resting in Peace Later

Hebrews 4

Today, we see RIP signs everywhere, especially during the pandemic. It's like saying, "Have a nice day." or "See ya later." to someone on the street. What does it mean, anyway? How do we know if people are resting in peace?

"Therefore, since the promise of entering his rest still stands, let us be careful that none of you be found to have fallen short of it."

Hebrews 4:1 NIV

Well, there appears to be some resting place or state after all, but a lot of people look to fall short of it.

""Enter through the narrow gate. For wide is the gate and broad is the road that leads to destruction, and many enter through it. But small is the gate and narrow the road that leads to life, and only a few find it."

Matthew 7:13-14 NIV

"For we also have had the good news proclaimed to us, just as they did; but the message they heard was of no value to them, because they did not share the faith of those who obeyed."

"Therefore since it still remains for some to enter that rest, and since those who formerly had the good news proclaimed to them did not go in because of their disobedience, God again set a certain day, calling it "Today." This he did when a long time later he spoke through David, as in the passage already quoted: "Today, if you hear his voice, do not harden your hearts."""

Hebrews 4:2, 6-7 NIV

It looks like the directions to rest and peace are still available now. But it's up to us to soften our hearts and pay attention.

Challenge

Let's go out today looking for God's direction, listening for his voice by either reading his word or listening to the godly people he has put in our lives. If our hearts are hard, it will bounce right off of us with little effect on us. But it says right here, that we can chose not to harden our hearts. Let's decide not to do that today.

Christ, Our Designated Hitter

Hebrews 5

In baseball, the designated hitter bats in place of the pitcher. It is hoped that his skill at batting will increase the teams chances at winning. Everyone on the team hopes that he will knock it out of the park and lift his team to victory.

In like manner, Jesus came to intercede for our team. We needed him to knock our sin outta the park and lead us to victory. We had been defeated by sin many times, no matter how hard we played, and we had no chance that we would make it into the post season. (heaven)

"Son though he was, he learned obedience from what he suffered and, once made perfect, he became the source of eternal salvation for all who obey him and was designated by God to be (designated) high priest in the order of Melchizedek."

Hebrews 5:8-10 NIV

Not only is Jesus our designated hitter representing us as an all star and player rep before the owner, he is also our designated player. When any player on our team is struggling, he goes to support them. If we strike out, he becomes our batting coach, and helps us with our swing, next time we're up to bat. He even gets all the players to pull together to help one another, and to help those who might want to join the team. He cheers everyone on knowing how great it will be in the post season when everyone comes together and celebrates with the owner.

He is always training his team to follow the rules and to do their very best giving their whole heart. That way everyone on board, gets stronger and better the longer they play for his team. Some of the mature players can even become pitch hitters when they are needed to help out a weak player. "But solid food is for the mature, who by constant use have trained themselves to distinguish good from evil."

Hebrews 5:14 NIV

Challenge

Let's go out today remembering that we have someone to stand up for us, someone to help us out and be close to us even if we've struck out a few times. He will take us all the way into the post season, if we stay close to him and follow his directions. A golden crown is reserved for us in the post season.

"I am coming soon. Hold on to what you have, so that no one will take your crown."

Revelation 3:11 NIV

Let's never forget that when it was his time to bat in our most important game, Jesus laid down a sacrifice so that we could run home with the winning run.

End of Morning Dives

Volume 1

Conclusion

Hope you have enjoyed your journey with Morning Dives and have deepened your faith in God and walk with him and Jesus. Be sure and join us again for Morning Dives Volume 2, The Beginning and the End. May God bless your efforts to wholeheartedly seek after him and some day be with him for Eternity.

The Beginning, and the End.

Start

"Now the Lord God had planted a garden in the east, in Eden; and there he put the man he had formed."

Genesis 2:8 NIV

Finish

"No longer will there be any curse. The throne of God and of the Lamb will be in the city, and his servants will serve him."

Revelation 22:3 NIV

"You will seek me and find me when you seek me with all your heart."

Jeremiah 29:13 NIV

Who's ready to Dive into Volume 2?

Special Note of Thanks

A special thanks to my wife and daughters for all their support and encouragement. Also to all my friends, brothers and sisters at church who helped inspire putting this book together. Most of all thanks to God for providing me so many blessings in life especially over the past 40 years, despite periods of struggle and unfaithfulness. I know that one day he will welcome me into his eternal realm, and if you will be faithful, I will gladly hold a place for you with your name on it. "Now there is in store for me the crown of righteousness, which the Lord, the righteous Judge, will award to me on that day—and not only to me, but also to all who have longed for his appearing."

2 Timothy 4:8

May this book inspire you on your journey of faith, so that one day you too will come and take your place.

Author Bio

D. C. Kinder grew up in Baltimore, Md., but attended colleges in Pa, Texas, Wisconsin, and Boston, Ma. Finally, in 1996, he achieved his Masters in English Teaching from Boston University's School of Education. From there, he taught college at Inha Univ. Of Inchon, South Korea.

Upon returning to the US after a year, he taught English for private schools in Florida and eventually began working for Broward County Public Schools, where he worked primarily with Special Ed students for 20 years. His literary style is influenced by Gary Larsen, the renown cartoonist, as well as Dr. Seuss, the well known poetic author.

He has two almost grown girls and plans on publishing several book series in the next few years focused on character development and education. Essential to his work is the inclusion of humor. The humor in most if Kinder's writing is what brings them to life and makes learning a truly fun experience.

Author's Favorites

Favorite Movies

Anything Marvel

Anything Harrison Ford

National Treasure

Rocky

Favorite Music

Greatest Showman Soundtrack

Any kind of Gospel

Can't Touch This

Like to Move It, Move It

Favorite Writers

Gary Larson

Dr. Seuss

JK Rowling

TV Shows

MacGyver

Gunsmoke

Andy Griffith

American Idol

America's Got Talent

Favorites on the Web🕸👤💻

Facebook

Youtube

Whatsapp

Favorite QR connections

Lesson

Site 1

Site 2

TUES. 8PM
US Eastern Time
Zoom Discussion

Favorite Photo

Sneak Peak into Vol 2

"A long time ago, in the same place where you are standing, God said, "Watch this," and with that, he made everything, and put everything in motion right up until you were born."

"On top of all that, he gave them the most awesome garden where they could live rent free with him and walk with him forever, no need to worry about paying bills, or growing old."

"Way back near the beginning, a Master of Scam got into Eden and got into a discussion with one of the residents named Eve. His goal was to convince her that she needed something that she didn't have."

www.ingramcontent.com/pod-product-compliance
Lightning Source LLC
LaVergne TN
LVHW091224150826
845673LV00003B/994

* 9 7 9 8 8 4 1 9 3 6 7 0 1 *